Spirit Guides, Angels, And Speaking with Source

The Angelic Collective of Xorbítal
Channelled by Brandon H. Bloom

Spirit Guides, Angels, And Speaking with Source

A channelled guide to begin expanding your connection and ability to speak with, and channel, those of the highest light who are here for the highest good, and hone your other gifts as well.

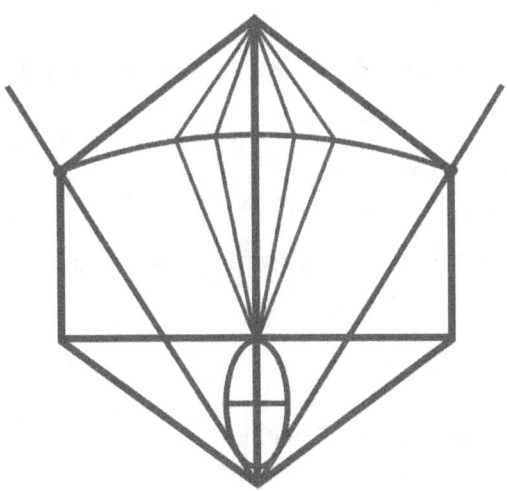

The Angelic Collective of Xorbítal
Channelled by Brandon H. Bloom

Copyright © 2020 by Brandon H. Bloom

All Rights Reserved. No part of this book may be reproduced, stored in a retrieval system, or transmitted in any form or by any means electronic, mechanical, photocopying, recording, or otherwise without written permission from the author, except in the case of brief quotations utilized in reviews or articles pertaining to the book.

It is the responsibility of the reader to discern how best to apply the information found within this book, and neither the author nor any publisher involved with the distribution of this book is legally responsible or liable for any reader or consumer of this book, including their actions, choices, and/or outcomes, for any reason. Reading this book, or using any of the information within it, is entirely at your own risk, and neither the author, nor the publisher assume any legal responsibility for your actions or outcomes. (Though truly, we are wishing you the best.)

Niether this book, nor the information it contains, is intended as a substitute for medical advice.

The symbol on the front cover, Vustá © 2020 by Brandon H. Bloom

Library of Congress Control Number: 2020916299

Paperback ISBN: 978-1-7355866-9-4
Ebook ISBN: 978-1-7355866-0-1

brandonhbloom.com

This book is dedicated to all who have aided me, in the highest and best ways, along my journey, and to all those for whom it is meant to reach. Sending Love.

Table of Contents

Introduction..1

Chapter 1: The Why and The Intention.........................9

Chapter 2: Honing In..15

Chapter 3: You Are Gifted...21

Chapter 4: Expanding Your Gifts................................27

Chapter 5: Energy...39

Chapter 6: Knowing..47

Chapter 7: Trusting...51

Chapter 8: Discernment..57

Chapter 9: Walk Your Path...61

Outro: Thank You...67

Further Information...69

Further Offerings...71

Blessings...73

Acknowledgements...75

About The Author...77

Introduction

DOWNLOADS AND BLESSINGS

Welcome, and prepare for an adventure, a journey into and through potentially new territory for you as an incarnate being on Earth. By purchasing this book, you have already set the intention to begin connecting more frequently and strongly with your guides, angels, Source, The Highest Light, and those who walk with you for your highest, greatest good, in the highest and best ways. You can consider the words contained in this book a download, and by that we mean you are receiving an energetic transmission on channelling (only what's of the highest light and for the highest good) and on speaking and otherwise communicating with your spiritual guidance team in whatever ways will work best for you, as each of you reading this are unique and will have a best way to communicate spiritually with those guiding you. You will also find you connect with differing beings. Many of you will find you naturally connect in with angelic beings and frequencies quite easily. Others of you, may lean towards Galactic messengers, dragons (they do exist), spirit animals, or other means of connecting with The Light. Source is all, and all stems from Source, so in truth, it is possible to connect directly to

Source and channel from there, speak to God, so to say. And seeing as God is all, Source is all, The Light, is all, in essence, you are never separated from God, from Source, from the Universe, and you are God, you are Source, you are the Universe. Your connection is inherent, a part of you. It may take practice, shifting beliefs out of the way, and time to develop, hone in on, and figure out what gifts you innately have and how best to work with them, however, this connection you have to Source, once discovered and utilized, over time, will grow stronger, more potent, and more readily accessible to you. All it takes is to start, to leap, to take the jump, and to do this, set the intention. We will provide you the words you can use as a jumping off point (Chapter 1), however, once you take that leap, and once the messages begin coming (and they WILL come), it is up to you to walk your best path, to hone your skills, and to develop a working relationship with your guides, intuitive faculties, and any other guidance systems you energetically utilize in navigating your life, living, and moving forward in the highest and best ways for you.

That is the message for the introduction. Within its words is the first transmission, which you have received in the highest and best ways and for the (and your) highest greatest good.

With highest divine love,
The Angelic Collective of Xorbítal through Brandon

"Now You Write," They (the angels and my guides) tell me, 'gesturing' towards me, and I say gesturing as they, in my 'mind's eye', in this instance, showed me a sort of image of angels motioning towards me, though in truth what they convey to me is also a deeper feeling, and a knowing, which goes along with the words, imagery, and any other sounds they add in, along with, sometimes, smells. An energetic sense. It's like when you walk into a room, and it feels happy, and you just know everyone's having a good time, and as you commingle you discover that's exactly what's been going on, or, less fun, it feels like there's something sour in the air, and as you investigate, you discover someone had just had a verbal fight or conflict. Many of you have likely met someone and instantly received a 'vibe' about them, a knowing about what they are like, deep down, and how they operate in general. I'm guessing that if you are reading this you are energetically sensitive, or identify as an empath, which to me, are really saying much the same thing. That being the case, you are likely familiar with feeling the energies of a person, place, or situation. Whether or not you've honed that gift into something that allows you to read people, places, or situations easily, if you needed to hone it in the first place, does not matter so much right now as the understanding that, often, when your guides communicate to you, there will be an energy along with the message. Your guides aren't limited to communicating to you any one way. Hence, what I was speaking about right after my guides told me to write the rest of this introduction: the energetic feeling of what my guides were conveying to me, along with the imagery and words. That's simply one example of my guides communicating to me that I can put into this book, and it happens all the time, every day, throughout the day, and it's extremely helpful. Communicating with people, going about your daily work life, knowing just what to say to a friend, knowing who to date and who to walk away from, and, of course larger life choices and directions. There are no limits to what your guides and angels, Source, and all those walking with you for your highest, greatest good, can help you with. This is more than a book about talking to guides, but is, rather, a book that can kickstart a world of opportunity and possibility where you can go further than ever before in your life and living with deeper knowing, and deeper assistance and support than you ever previously thought possible. Please trust the unfoldment of your journey, and know you are supported deeply, you have been drawn to this book for a reason (or vice versa, perhaps the book found its way to you), and you will get all you need as you move forward on your journey, and any gaps you are left with as you read will be filled in by your guides themselves, by your higher self, Source, or whoever you communicate with, as we can not do the work for you, but can open you up, kick start the process, and wish you well on your way to opening up, unfolding, and going deeper into your communications with the divine.

What is Channelling? And Who is Xorbítal?

In case you were wondering, "Who is Xorbítal?" Allow me to talk about that briefly. I began channelling more consciously in 2017, though, looking back, it's definitely happened throughout childhood to greater or lesser degrees. In my experience, and with what I get, channelling is, essentially, The Divine working through you, speaking through you, or delivering messages through you for the highest good. This can show up as angels working and speaking through you, or providing you messages for you to relay to others, Source itself, Spirit guides (of the highest light and here for the, and your, highest good), Ascended Masters for some, and the like. It is higher/highest consciousness, all knowing, infinitely wise, infinitely intelligent, and unconditionally loving, speaking or working through you. That or better. Some examples of different ways channelling can occur or bring forth or birth creations into the world are through art, painting, music, poetry, various healing modalities, symbols that have energetic impacts, or even physical actions, such as channelled massages (not to be confused with messages, and yes channelled massages are some of the best massages ever). Automatic writing, (which includes typing) is another way to channel, which is how most of this book has been written, as it is a channelled work. (All of it, I just heard.) When it comes to channeling, or speaking with your guides, you can truly be guided through, and with, anything. As you progress and are lead by the Universe through your journey, you will be guided and shown a deeper intuitive understanding of what channelling is to you, that or better.

    A quick addendum, channelled works and messages often are accompanied by an energetic transmission, effect, and/or download, which works for the highest good of the recipient of the channelled work, or those who come into contact with it, in whatever ways are for the highest good of each respectively, should it be in their highest good. I always ask for what's highest and best, as Source is infinite, infinitely intelligent, infinitely wise, and it knows best, which means it is infinitely capable of delivering what's highest and best, even better than what can be imagined. When you encounter Xorbítal talking about this book being like an attunement to channelling, this is, in part, what they are referring to, though, with this work, it is also more than that. They speak more about this in the outro.

After becoming more proficient, with more and more instances of channelling through messages from my guides, from the Divine, from the angels and/or Source occurring, (they were always for the highest good, accurate, on the money, even about future events), I began to wonder if there was a name, as other channelers out there frequently had a name for who, or what, they were channelling. The answer is no, not really, names don't matter so much up there, but after I asked about it directly, after I had just channelled a message, they gave me a name with the spelling: "The Angelic Collective of Xorbítal". For a bit more context, I had been, (and still am) channelling through symbols (one of which is on the cover of this book) for a language/healing modality for which I received the name Valeyu-Mí. I had been channelling them through for about a year at that point, and the names of the symbols frequently included accents over specific letters. I'm getting Xorbítal, with the accent over the 'i' was a nod and a wink to that. A little while after receiving the name, while channelling for a friend of mine who's extremely intuitive and an amazing energy worker, and who, at this point, is beginning to channel a lot herself, she asked, "Uhh, Brandon, do you know who your guides are?" At which point I said something along the lines of, "Well, I'm pretty sure they're a bunch of angels." To which she responded, "Yeah, I'm feeling some Archangel Metatron in there, some Archangel Michael..." and she went on to list various archangels and angels. When I inquire to my guides now, "who is Xorbítal?" I get, "All the Archangels and then some. All for the highest good."

When it comes to channelling your guides, delving into what I get about it, you are not limited to channelling just one being, collective of beings, etc. I can channel, and have channelled Source directly. I've also channelled dragons before (all for the highest good), and talk with them quite frequently. I've seen them around quite a bit and have asked for there assistance in energy work sessions and daily life with great results. If you're into ascended masters you can channel them. The friend I spoke about in the preceding paragraph channels and speaks with Quan Yin to amazing effect. There are no limits, for it is about what resonates with you, and what you connect with. The thing is, when channelling what's of the highest light and for the highest, greatest good to be channelled, so frequently you are also channelling from a higher part of yourself, for Source is all, myself and yourself included, and you and I are also Source, so, in effect I am all of it, you are all of it, we are all of it, and we are one. That's the short of it, at least. I remember at one point, my guides went to show me something. It was a vision or visual of sorts, and it was an image they frequently utilized to communicate with me of a large group of angels standing about amongst each other facing me, however, they showed the image, then they 'peeled it away' so to speak, to reveal Source. Take from that what you will, or what you are guided to receive from it, however, to me, in a sense, there is more than one avenue to connect with Source, The LIGHT that is all, even though you are all directly connected to Source, which is, of course, infinite. Whether it be through angels, your guides, directly to Source, what's behind it is truly Divine, Higher up, so to speak, and for the highest good, of course, inherently. Everything is one.

    A quick side note, when I'm channelling directly, so often when I would typically refer to myself as 'I' in conversation, 'I' will instead say, "we", for it is Source, the Angels, Xorbítal speaking through me for the highest good, so to honor that the term "we" is introduced instead. Brandon is conscious while he channels, he hears what we are saying through him and/or what we are urging him to say, we can simultaneously be speaking through him and to him in different capacities, showing him images, intuitive visuals, and simultaneously speaking through him to the listener and to him to aid in his delivery of the messages we are speaking through him, for we are not limited and neither is he, and neither are you. It is interesting for Brandon to talk or type about himself in third person, for we are speaking through him, and he is conscious of what is being said and/

or written, but we have guided him to step aside his ego and allow us to channel through him in the highest and best ways, regardless of how we refer to him or 'us'.

(I guess they really wanted to channel a direct example and explanation there midway through that first sentence of the preceding paragraph and onward. I'll leave all of that there as a written example of what was being discussed. I do want to add though, you can make requests of how you are referred to by your guides when you channel. You can move in different directions with it, though as they did for me, they will likely guide you through the highest and best ways for you to do it for you. Additionally, there are instances where I'm channelling and/or receiving information for people who are not used to encountering direct channelling, for instance, my guides/Source, the angels, will be feeding me the information, messages, words to use, and delivery methods while I'm speaking to someone at work, and while I'm channelling it all, I'm not in full on, eyes closed, guides speaking through me mode. In those instances, even if I do begin directly channelling, if it is in the highest good or better for Xorbítal, Source, my guides, etc., to channel through me but for them to use the terms 'I' or 'me' instead of 'we', they will do so. If the recipient of the messages is not accustomed to channelling, and/or the location is somewhere such as a place of work and other people are around, my guides will use discretion and discernment in how the message is delivered, as they are infinite, infinitely intelligent, infinitely wise, and they know exactly what is best for each moment. That all comes down to trusting in how they are urging the message to be delivered, for they can and will guide you in all of that as well, if you will allow it, and, potentially, depending on who you are, ask for it.)

This is, of course, all information that will apply more if you plan on, or begin to be guided to channel more directly for others. For those simply wishing to communicate with your spiritual guidance team, rest assured you will get all of the information, downloads, and upgrades needed to sufficiently begin undertaking that endeavor. It will show up for each of you, respectively, in the highest and best ways for it to show up for you, for it is infinite intelligence which guides all of this, which is all of this, including life itself. You have nothing to fear in this process, especially as you set your boundaries and intentions through your words, written, spoken aloud, or to yourself.

May you be blessed as you unfold and open up, may you receive all you need from this book and then some, all for your, and the, highest good, and may it lead you to where you need to go, to being who you are meant to be, to being all the best you can be, that or better, should it be in your, and the, highest good, for your, and the, highest good. Amen. Thank you. Let's begin.

May the highest and best downloads, activations, and energies flow to you, work for your highest greatest good, or otherwise work in the highest and best ways for you as you read this book or have it in your vicinity. May this book work in the highest and best ways for you, doing for you whatever would be for your highest, greatest good, through the words it contains, the transmissions it sparks, or through any other means that would be for the, and your, highest good. That or better, should it be in the highest good. Thank you Source for making it so.

(A quick note for clarification: while the beginning of the introduction was channelled, with the rest of the introduction being written more by me (Brandon, though they still guided me through it), all of the rest of this book is channelled excepting for the "further offerings", "acknowledgements", and "about the author" sections, though again, I was guided through all of those as well. Thank you. I hope you get all the best from this!)

Chapter 1

THE WHY, AND THE INTENTION

We're hoping you read the introduction. (There's a download in there!) We recommend you go read it right now if you haven't, however, if you refuse, worry not, you'll get all you need as you read forward.

So, that question, "Why channel?" "Why talk to my guides?" "Why talk to angels?" We understand humans sometimes ask these questions, and indeed, it makes sense, no one wants to waste their time. We assure you, undertaking this journey, should it be one you are called to, will only be a boon to your life and living, and a great one at that. It is one of the best things you can do for yourself, cultivate your awareness and your knowing, and talking to spirit guides, to angels, to Source and the Universe, is a great way to open up to your innate Divine self and knowing. As you open up, you realize things are light hearted 'up there' (in quotation marks because it is all ONE), we crack jokes to you, we send you images and visuals that make you laugh, we inspire you to lighten up, for if The Divine cracks jokes, so too can you in your daily life, though we recommend you do so without denigrating yourself or one another. As you realize the true nature of The Divine, it becomes easier to embody that, to be a conduit of that, to be one with your Divine nature, for indeed, you are Source as much as anyone else is, even if you have not realized it yet. And as you open up to your true Divine nature, you become more you, who, and what, you actually are. For you are Source, you are the Universe, you are Light, here, incarnate on the planet of Earth, and you chose to be here, and this does not make Brandon or anyone else any less Source, any less The Universe, any less The Light, but rather points to the inner divinity of all beings, which points to this connection of yours you will be developing to communicate with The Light as being not just a fancy schmancy trick, but a real, true, deep, inherent part of you, and of everyone and anyone who chooses to acknowledge that this part of them is there and real.

You could say it is more natural to channel, to talk to your guides, than to not, as this utilizes an inherent part of you, and just because others don't, or haven't yet, acknowledged this part of them doesn't mean it isn't there, and doesn't mean it isn't more real than all the stories, made up, about how life works, that have proven to be false, and to have not worked, that for some reason, some people still tell themselves.

All that to say, this journey, this beginning to talk to your guides, no matter how slowly (or quickly) it unfolds, is one that will help you, not only spiritually, but, potentially, in most all areas of your life, and this is for a number of reasons:

1. As you begin to entrain to a higher frequency, a divine frequency, which channelling, and talking to your guides and angels, most certainly helps you to do, your raise in frequency will impact every area of your life and living, as those areas of your life will begin to upgrade as you do, will raise in frequency along with you. New people will show up as you grow, new, more aligned living and work situations will magically appear as you become a truer version of you, and new callings and opportunities will begin to present themselves to you as you expand.

2. You will receive guidance directly in all areas of your life, including, but not limited to, romance, work life, family situations, friendships, living situations, sexy time (yes, you can be guided through sexy time for optimal pleasure), spiritual development, eating and nutrition, exercise, what works for you (in any given area or situation) and what doesn't work for you. As you learn to trust and open up to this guidance, and learn to rely on it as needed, suddenly your choices become more aligned, more in alignment with the truths of what is actually happening in your life, and you will be able to navigate your life and living with greater ease, clarity, and certainty, where it is appropriate and necessary especially, as well as where and how you will welcome it and *receive it*.

3. You will always be supported, and know it, and hear it. They will always be with you, loving you, encouraging you, guiding you, and you will be able to hear them guiding you on, encouraging you, to the last second of your life. They will tell you what is up, in general, specifically, and in all ways that would be best for you, because they love you unconditionally, no matter what you do, no matter what you say, no matter the trails you choose to take, and should you be open to it they will guide you so long as you are listening, and even if you are not, they will still hold space for you until you are ready. For that is the way of love. And your highest and best guidance always comes from a place of highest divine love, from a pure place of the highest sort, from a love that knows no bounds, from an infinite love.

In a sense, your guides are you, the love that you are, and they are here to guide you through heaven and 'hell', through thick or thin, through whatever you encounter, through whatever this life throws at you, because you are worth it, you are the divine incarnate, and they won't let your life go to waste if you won't. (Not that any life is a waste, simply that *you are more than worth guiding, for you are infinitely worthy in the best ways, seeing as You are Source and Source is*

You.)

This guidance, this connection with the Divine, is obviously a boon to your life, logically and pragmatically, spiritually, in fun ways, in serious ways, and in all ways, all for the highest, greatest good.

If you've felt called to read this, you likely already have a why for beginning to talk to your guides, your highest self, to begin communicating with the Divine directly, even if it's subconscious or energetic, even if it's just a pull towards this type of communication with the infinite that you may or may not be able to fully explain in words. So from here, let's move into intention, to begin, to kickstart, to kick off your channelling and communication with your spiritual guidance team, all for the highest good, in the highest and best ways.

To do this, all you need to 'do', is *ASK*. For The Universe, The Light, God, Source, Allah, whatever your term for the Divine which is infinite, and which is all, is you, and you are it, and from that point of recognition you can realize it always, <u>always</u> hears you, for it is you, it is the words you speak, the molecules in the air that carry the vibrations of your voice, the thoughts running through your brain, and beyond. As such, it understands infinitely well what you are intending with your thoughts, actions, words, and beyond; it understands where you are coming from. From this understanding, all you need to 'do' to manifest, to kickstart a process (at least energetically), is to **_ASK_**.

So, center yourself, ground, get into a meditative state, jump into your heart, and from this pure place, this purity of what you truly are, who you truly be, ask. If you would like an example to spring off of, we will provide one in the next paragraph, but understand as you develop your intuition, as you talk with your guides more and communicate with the Divine, you will begin to get your own messages, intentions, ways of doing things that work best for you, so use these intentions and words as a springboard to begin uncovering what works best for you, for your, and the, highest, greatest good.

Ready? Here we go:

Universe, Source, Divine, I know you hear me, and I ask sincerely to, in the highest and best ways, begin channelling, to hear from my guides and/or highest self, to begin communicating with the Divine, The Infinite, in the highest and best ways for me to do so, whatever that looks like, whatever would be highest and best, for me, and I ask only to communicate with and channel what is of the highest light, what is for my, and the, highest greatest good, channelling through what's in the highest greatest good for whoever I am channelling for, receiving the highest and best accurate information about what I'm channelling, downloading, or receiving information about, and I ask to work with and develop these gifts you are bestowing upon me, and/or which I already had access to latently, in the highest and best ways, all of this, and/or better, for the, and my, highest greatest good, in the highest and best ways, amen. Thank you, thank you, thank you.

If you are energetically sensitive, sit with any energetic shifts you feel occurring for yourself and in your life after setting this intention. Trust the timing of what unfolds, and trust it will unfold in the highest and best ways for you. You can ask that it all unfolds in the highest and best ways for you, however, seeing as The Universe is you, and you are The Universe, and The Universe is unconditionally loving, The Universe is always working and looking out for you, and your highest good, in the highest and best ways. As you begin talking to your guides, and channelling, all in the highest and best ways, and for the highest, greatest good, you will begin to receive accurate explanations for why and how things are unfolding the way that they are, which will lead to greater peace and serenity in your life, seeing as you will be able to go beyond the surface, beyond what seems to be reality, or what seems to be the case, to attain a deeper truth about what is going on, with a person, a situation, with life, with the world, and from there, you will be able to move forward, to rest, to recalculate and recalibrate with greater ease than ever before, because you will know the truth.

    Your intuition and energetic sensitivity, which feed into one another greatly, combined with channelling and speaking with angels and your guides (which can be the same thing), will lead to an ultimate combination of truth seeking and finding, in which your awareness will skyrocket, your spiritual abilities and gifts will blossom and bloom tremendously, and in which, your spiritual growth will become unbound, as the lies or half-truths some teachers spread, intentionally or unintentionally, will not fool you any longer. In fact, nothing will fool you any longer after a time of developing and acquainting yourself with your guidance systems.

Now that you have acquainted yourself with setting intentions, with the impacts they can have, and with the benefits of channelling, speaking to your guides and/or angels, and developing a working relationship with the Divine, let's move on to the next chapter.

May you be guided lovingly and clearly, in the highest and best ways. May you expand in the ways you <u>truly</u> wish to and are meant to with ease and grace. All that or better, in the highest and best ways, should it be in the highest good, thank you Source for making it so.

Chapter 2

HONING IN

So, you've chosen to take the leap, you've chosen to set an intention, and perhaps you took it a step further, developing a ritual that went along with your setting of intention, whether that was prayer in a particular area, lighting a candle, meditating with a certain incense, or whatever resonates and works best *for you*. You might now be asking… "Now what?"

Well, the first thing we want to say is: patience. There is divine timing with everything, and you can trust your channelling, gifts, and communications with your guides will unfold more consciously for you in the near future, if not now. It is likely as you have been thinking or feeling called to communicate with your spirit guides and/or angels, they have been there aiding in facilitating your desire for that all along, or otherwise guiding you to uncover your natural desire and knack for it.

Take a moment to sit and think, see if any images or memories jump out at you as you read these words: at any point in time throughout your life, have there been any voices in your head that didn't 'sound' like yours, or that felt different than what typically 'plays' in your head? We do not speak of any disorders, for our follow up question is this: did what those voices tell you turn out to be true or helpful? Your angels have been around you this whole time. Did you ever receive any flashes of intuition, an insight that just hit you instantly, an image, a phrase, or a word shown to you in your minds eye? For your angels and guides do not only speak with words, but can communicate visually through stationary or moving visuals and images, through feeling and energetic sensations, and also through 'downloading' instant knowings to you where you just know. Sometimes what they show you is overlayed on top of your 'ordinary' life experiences of vision. Perhaps you have felt urges or random compulsions to say or do a certain thing to or for someone, and it turned out to be just what they needed to hear, or just what needed to be done for that person, in just the right ways. Oftentimes, communication from your guides, the angels, or even The Universe itself is a combination of all of the above and then some, for there are no limitations to how your guides may communicate to you, or even through you, and they will do so in the best ways that work for you, *especially if you ask.*

We say all this because it is entirely possible your angels have already been communicating with you, even if you hadn't realized it. If any particular memories, images, or flashes of insight occurred to you while you were reading the paragraph above this one, that is your intuition showing you where your guides have been trying to communicate with you, whether you listened to them or knew what it was or not. Now, the methods employed by your guides and angels may change, grow, and evolve as you are ready for it, and perhaps reading this book, and setting the intention to begin channelling and speaking with them directly will open the pathway for the next phase in your evolution with communication with your angels and guides, however, even if they have already been speaking with you directly, prepare for that method of communication to grow stronger, more consistent, and more connected in the highest and best ways. For opening this book begins a download, an upgrade, for the one reading it, facilitated for the highest good, by Spirit, by Source, and simply by sitting with this book, reading its words, you receive the information <u>Divinely</u>, *energetically,* that allows you to begin channelling and speaking with your spirit guides, angels, and/or, otherwise, the highest and best beings for you to be speaking with, in the highest and best ways, and only for the highest good. You are reading this book for a reason. Please receive the downloads and upgrades for your highest good, and trust that only what's for your highest good will come to you. We, Xorbítal, and The Angels will ensure it.

Reading this book is like an attunement to channelling and speaking with your guides, all in the highest and best ways and for your, and the, highest greatest good. So simply by reading these words, you are honing in on your connection, an inherent part of you. If you choose to keep going, then this will strengthen, and you will become more aware of your channelling, of your ability to communicate with The Divine, and your ability to discern between your thinking and your reception of Divine information and messages will unfold beautifully, if it is not already strong. If you are already aware of your channelling, then prepare for it to get better, easier.

Another way, to solidify these intentions and put these downloads to good use, is to develop a practice for your channelling and communication with your guides. Whether this is channelling as you write in a notebook, recording a video of yourself (as you get more comfortable having your guides channelling through you), or simply sitting in a meditative state with a candle or some incense each week, or day, whatever feels right for you, simply taking time to dedicate to your channelling practice, or to set aside time to sit and listen for your guides and angels, will allow you to open up to them at a steady pace, and allows you to develop rapidly, as consistently showing up gives the Universe ample opportunity to provide you with the growth and upgrading you desire.

Take time to listen. That is what the aforementioned practices will do for you, is provide time and space for you to listen and expand your awareness surrounding messages you are receiving. It becomes easy over time, and we will not limit you, we will not say it won't be easy for you to communicate with your guides and angels throughout your daily life, even in the midst of a hectic schedule or busy time at work, for it is very possible to do so with ease. The bottom line is expanding awareness and receptivity to channelling, and listening to your angels and guides so that you are more aware of when it is occurring and how you best operate with it. We will not say there is any one way, for there are many. The important piece is, is it working for you? Are you expanding and growing? Is it getting easier?

That is why we say, do not limit yourself to what is written in this book, or what you read or hear elsewhere, for there is a way that works for you, and *you know what that is*, for you are the Universe, and the Universe is you, so there is definitely a part of you that knows, which is why we encourage you to *ask for it, so that it comes to you more easily*. Getting in touch with your own knowing can be so empowering to one on their spiritual path or journey, whatever you call it, because it allows you to know what is truly true for you, without you being pulled around by what anyone else is saying. This is why we encourage you to embark on this path of self-discovery and opening to The Divine more fully for your highest good, to bring more truth and light to this world, straight from Source, The Divine, itself.

Again, we offer you this tool: *ask*. Ask to open up in the highest and best ways, ask for your abilities to channel and connect with your guides, with Source, and communicate to become easier and more consistent, to expand and develop in the highest and best, easiest ways for you, at whatever pace(s) would be highest and best for you, with greatest ease and comfort for your growth and expansion, for this practice will, it is highly likely, transform you in the highest and best ways. You will have more Divine energy flowing through you, you will be at a higher vibration, you will find yourself a more knowing, wise, kind, and loving person, with more peace and calm in you, around you, and in your life. It may not show up all at once, but as you continue to entrain to The Divine, to Source, to higher vibrations, you, and everyone and everything around you will begin to shift in ways you can not imagine. Trust that the Universe wishes to give, is unconditionally loving, and wants great things for you. So these changes will only be for the best, or will lead, at the very least, to better for you. You simply need only to let go, trust, and receive this better. This will occur for you at whatever rates are best for you. *Just keep going. Don't be afraid, please trust the Divine, The Universe, this life.*

Don't be afraid, if things don't happen right away, though they will for many of you. They will happen *if you keep going.* If you *keep showing up.* If you *keep trying.* The 'trick' is to *keep going.* If it is not yet clear, it will get there if you keep showing up and keep going, and keep asking, and keep moving. If it is not yet there, it will be, trust and *keep going.* This isn't a blender you bought from the hardware store, this is an intuitive, divine, beautiful gift you are developing, and we will not say it always takes time, for some of you are extremely gifted and will find great ease right off the bat. The point we are looking to make, is that you must go within and discover, uncover, and develop this gift, hone it in, keep going with it, even if it takes a while, though again, it might come quickly. Once you get going, then it will be easier to pick up the pace, however, trust your unfoldment. The divine knows what is right for you. Your gifts are there. Hone them.

Once you set an intention, the right people, places, things, and messages, one way or another, will begin falling into place to assist you in going where you are meant to go, for the Universe is all. It is your 'job' then, to *go that direction,* keep 'following the bread crumbs' The Universe is giving you, (though it is likely to be *way* more than 'bread crumbs'), keep taking action as you are guided and lead to do, and The Universe will continue to guide you through the highest and best ways for you to take, should you be willing, and open, to taking those ways.

May you be blessed in the highest and best ways, with a quick and fast development of your channelling gifts and abilities, and with the ability to speak with and hear from your guides clearly and easily. May all this occur with ease and grace, in a way that's for your highest good. All of this, should it be in the, and your, highest good, thank you.

Chapter 3

YOU ARE GIFTED

You have undoubtedly heard you are special, or different in some way, or felt that way yourself, even if you couldn't quite place your finger on what exactly that was. Perhaps you are more in tune than you realize, more aware. Perhaps you are kinder, more gentle than other people around you, even if you don't readily realize it. (And it's time to *start* realizing it, and actively living more aware of who you are, and how you are gifted). Perhaps you just *know* things, or find yourself feeling like something is going to happen, something is coming up, and then it happens.

Perhaps you *see* things. And, mind you, if any memories or recollections of incidences from your life are flashing up for you as you read these words, that is an intuitive message, or recollection, regarding what we are talking about here, that you yourself have undergone, experienced, or otherwise utilized in your daily life at one point or another. So yes, as you read, you are intuitively being shown what we are talking about here.

Perhaps you *hear* things, whispers, or voices that deliver you messages, either for yourself or others, which may be accommodated by little nudges, urges, or <u>compulsions</u> to do something, or say something in particular to someone who needs to hear just what you are saying. Sometimes this is to kickstart events, awakenings, or simply The Universe answering a prayer for someone who has desperately prayed for an answer, an assistance, or a kind word. You are one with the Universe, so of course, as you awaken to who you really are, and what you really are, you will find yourself being naturally drawn to help others in ways that are fulfilling and naturally rewarding to you, which suit your gifts and talents, as the Universe is the perfect match maker for your dreams, your gifts, your abilities, and what fills you up, and who is best for you to be around, for the Universe is you, and you are the Universe, and as such, the Universe knows you, and where you actually are, infinitely well. It can't mess it up. You are being Divinely watched over, cultivated to be who you are, and you do it naturally, for nature is *always* coming into balance, always refining into new and better orders. You can trust this infinite intelligence, for it is you. It makes up all.

You will find also, as you awaken to what is going on around you, that the Universe works through *everyone*, all of the time, through what they say, what they do, and sometimes the main factor 'separating' the 'awake' and the 'asleep' is who is aware of when the Universe is working through them, and/or the others around them. *Hint, it is always, for the Universe is all, <u>however,</u> there are certain times when it becomes blatant, and these are the main points we want you to focus on.

So this channelling, this talking with your guides and angels, this talking to Source, talking to God, is simply a more direct way for the Universe to work through you for the highest greatest good. Seeing as you are God, and God is you, Source is you, and you are Source, you have the power to set the intentions regarding how this shows up for you, but you can not 'divorce' yourself from the Universe, because the Universe is what you are, not to say you aren't beyond the Universe, simply that you are one with all. Your connection to all, your infiniteness is what allows these infinite possibilities regarding receiving Divine messages, enacting Divine Will, stepping out of 'what was possible before' into your unlimited capabilities to shape shift reality, to change the very basis of what was once considered possible through your intentions, through your manifesting, and through the unveiling of your gifts and abilities, which are quite readily a natural extension of the nature of your true being. You are infinite. You are not limited. You can transcend perceived limitations to begin knowing and perceiving well beyond what you thought was possible, even those of you who are well learned and practiced.

The point we are making is that *everyone is gifted.* Everyone, much like everything, stems from Source. Everyone has access, potentially easy access, to this unlimited, infinite Source of all, which means everyone can develop and hone their abilities, shine their light, wake up, become more energetically sensitive (this is a good thing, as it parallels becoming more aware), and everyone has a way that best works for them. A 'path' that best suits them. A 'way things look' for them, even if it's Jesus, or *totally different* than what you would expect, for The Light, Source, The Infinite will meet people where they are at, and the messages of light that come through will inherently be the same, *so long as those people are setting the intentions and genuinely coming from a connected place, genuinely channelling the Divine, what is of the highest light and for the highest good.* A being who identifies as Christian coming from a *genuinely connected* place who has *honed their gifts* will in general 'get along with', or find many commonalities in what feels right to them as a being who identifies as a New Ager who is coming from a *genuinely connected* place or *genuinely connected being* who identifies as an atheist (it humors us to type that), for the 'belief system' might accommodate the *packaging* of the message differently, but the inherent essence of the messages, so long as egos are stepped aside, and truth is pouring through, will be similar enough, and will not contradict, *at heart.* Self-identification at these instances can be seen for what it is: egoic. The labels do not exist outside the mind. For one can put labels and words on connection, on channelling, and on gifts, but in truth, these things are beyond any one religion, any one 'belief structure', for this transcends human-made structures of belief, or, put differently, it is beyond the stories humans tell themselves to explain how things work. If we were to get to the heart, it is because *in these instances, we do not have* to seek stories to explain things, for we embody, we <u>are</u> how these 'things' work. Even if we provided an explanation, the truth is, these 'things' simply are. These gifts are potent, they work, they exist. No matter your framework. Step into your infiniteness. Step into your knowing.

So when we tell you, "You are Gifted." You are. You're here for a reason, and it's time now to own it. You are here with your gifts, and it is time to claim them, to see them as they are, work with them, hone them in, *become more aware of when you are already using them, for you have worked with them, at least on and off, your whole life.* Psychic abilities, intuition 'on steroids', channelling accurate information about the future, about people you've never physically met, channelling information for another about their past experiences that reveals truths that others had attempted to obscure to the person you are now channelling for, *all of this and more* is **now** available to you, and previously has been, and you simply need to hone it in. Develop, expand, remove blockages, shift beliefs, whatever it takes to unveil this truth, that you can do these things, it is still possible for you to unveil these truths, gifts, and abilities. New ones might show up. Things you didn't expect might simply *be there* one day as you upgrade and develop. You will shift and change and grow, and your gifts and abilities might also evolve as you do, however, you can trust that it will be easy for you to flow with your ever evolving needs and abilities as you walk this 'path', this 'journey', this opening and awakening. For you will be more in tune, with yourself, with your energies, with the Universe, with what's happening around you, *than ever before,* at least this lifetime. :)

This is where we provide a simple strategy to honing in your gifts and abilities. It is like riding a bike: with practice, with repeated attempts, with showing up over and over again, you will eventually *begin having the experiences with your gifts you need in order to begin pedaling on your own.* And once you do, your own intuition and expanding abilities will lead you down the pathways you need to take to keep going and growing, leading you to the resources, people, friends, roommates, jobs, co-workers, teachers, etc. that will best serve you. You can also trust *The Universe itself* will bring you all you need at the same time. This 'dance' will aid your evolution tremendously, so we urge you to trust your guides, trust your gifts, trust you, and *trust life and the Universe to bring you all you need.*

Should it be in the, and your, highest good, we ask that the highest potential of your gifts is realized fully in the highest and best ways as soon as would be in your highest good, at whatever speed would be highest and best for you. Thank you Source for bringing about the full realization of the highest potential of the gifts of the one reading this passage, that or better.

Chapter 4

EXPANDING YOUR GIFTS

What we first want to point you towards is your awareness. It is your awareness that will tell you, urge you to realize when you are utilizing one of these gifts of yours, whether it be channelling, intuition, knowing/claircognizance, or any other innate, beautiful, amazing gift you may have, even if we have not yet, or don't, touch upon it directly in this book. If you are starting from square one, if you are relatively new to all of this, basic mindfulness will be of great value to you, and this is generally cultivated through mindfulness meditation. Granted, mindfulness meditations are simply one method of cultivating mindfulness, for mindfulness is simply *observing*, 'stepping back', so to speak and realizing all of what is going on around you, becoming more aware of your awareness, in a sense, as well as what is within your awareness. We understand, like Brandon was early on in his 'journey' with all of this, when others say things, things like, "find your center", or 'step back and observe', some of you may find yourself asking, "what does that even mean?". We are getting that *all of you* who read this book will be sensitive, energetically. You may call it 'empathicness', or identify as an empath, but more in alignment with what is actually going on, you are picking up on the energy around you, waking up to your sensitivity. You are energetically sensitive. And with this knowing, with this realization that you are feeling energies, if you were not already aware, we can further explain that everything is energy, your states of being, your experiences, and that anything and everything is accessible, energetically, to an energetically sensitive and aware being, because energetically, time and space are not limitations. This is to say, it is entirely possible to *feel into* what tomorrow will bring, how your friend across the world is doing, or to feel into what certain states of being are like. If you are unsure of where to begin with all of this, we introduce, or rather, re-introduce the tool of asking. Seeing as Source, The Universe, The Light, The Creator, is infinite, and you are infinite, and Source is you and you are Source, it is entirely possible for you to make any request, set any intention, and through this infinite Source, which always hears you, for it *is* you, the request will be granted. *Ask and you will receive, (always for the highest good.)* Bear in mind, Source is infinitely intelligent, and it is you, your heart, what makes up your thoughts and words, and is, and knows, *everything,* as it is all, so you can trust it knows the intricacies of how you work, and is not confused by your language or choice of words. That is to say, *it knows what's in your heart and soul.* It knows what you are truly asking. It is about the intention first, words are secondary. Seeing as states of being are energetic, and Source is infinite, is everything, (everywhere), and can provide, infinitely any energy at any place, at any time upon your request/intention, should it be in the highest good, you can simply ask Source/The Universe, "I ask to experience what mindfulness is like for the next 30 seconds starting… now!" The Universe will bring you that experience in whatever ways would be best for you for that 30 seconds. (You can set a timer if it helps you.) That is correct, Source can bring you to a particular state of being, simply by your asking for it. It is all energy.

    Allow us to demonstrate. Take a moment to feel how you are doing, where you are at, and a bit of what your surroundings are like, then, when you are ready, read the next sentence, and feel free to set the intention you receive what's in your highest greatest good to receive from it and the intentions it holds, all for the highest good.

In the highest and best ways, should it be in the highest good, we ask that when you finish reading the last word of this sentence, you are grounded, brought fully present, and brought to a state of total awareness for however long would be for your highest, greatest good, thank you Source for doing so for the reader, that or better.

Did you feel that shift?

Working with your sensitivity and your questions, you can now step into any state, experience anything you'd like to experience, energetically, simply upon request to Source, to the Universe, or to whatever higher power you ascribe to. It is that simple.

So, we will work with this power of intention setting to expand your awareness to encompass the use of your gifts. Simply request, aloud, or written:

Universe, in the highest and best ways, I ask to become fully aware of what gifts I have, how best to use them, and, if I've already been working with them, I ask to become more fully aware of when it is that I am using them so that I can work with them more consciously in the future, should it be in the highest good, and my highest good, thank you!

Once it is requested, life will take care of it. This is basic manifestation, for once you ask, or make a request of Source or the Universe, once you write it down with the intention it shows up, **it will show up.** Life and the Universe are infinitely intelligent, and know just how to bring things to you, and in fact, may have had something to do with you asking all along, considering The Universe *is* you, and *you are the Universe.* Once it's written down, it is coming. You may see signs or synchronicities around you regarding the manifestation. For instance, if you write down "love" in your notebook to manifest more love in your life, and are open to that showing up in the highest and best ways for you, you may start to notice the word "love" around you in your life more often. It may flash by on the side of a semi-truck trailer that pulls around the corner as you step outside of a store, or you may overhear it in conversations you walk by, the word, or a sentence where someone is talking about love entering their life. This synchronicity tells you the Universe is bringing your manifestation to you, and that you are on track to receive it. Also, once it shows up, don't be surprised if you get some sort of validation that it has arrived. Perhaps, if you were to ask for love, and it showed up, someone will up and tell you, "It looks like love has found you!" Once this new love shows up for you.

So don't be alarmed if you begin seeing the word awareness, or mindfulness, more frequently in your life after asking for it, or perhaps phrases, images, or messages about gifts may begin showing up around you. It depends on your personal workings with the Universe, what you've honed in with the Universe. Once you gain an understanding of a sign, the Universe will incorporate that sign into your life to communicate with you. Please trust your understandings and trust your intuition regarding the signs the Universe will begin sending your way, if it hasn't already. The Universe is infinitely intelligent, and it is all, so after a time of working with the Universe in this way, synchronicity will simply become a way of life. We do want to add in that some signs will, in fact, point towards something coming up in your future, beyond the realm of manifestations. So if a sign appears that, to you, does not yet make sense, for instance, if a specific word, phrase, or color begins showing up over and over in various facets, trust that all will be revealed to you in divine timing regarding the sign. In essence, we are urging you to *pay attention* when it comes to things showing up for you.

We provide this extra information on manifestation for it will allow you greater freedom in working with the Universe in creating the life you would most like to live. It is also a help with kickstarting your journey, and expanding upon it, when it comes to talking with your guides.

We will use this vantage point to jump into a more coherent strategy on gift development:

1. *Intentions*

Please remember the power of setting intentions. The more acquainted you become with setting intentions, noticing their impact/feeling the energetic shifts that accompany them, and seeing the results, the easier it will be to begin expanding in whatever direction you choose, though of course, you will be guided accordingly towards what is best for you and what belongs with you as your abilities to communicate with the angels and your guides, with God, with Source, improve, if you are not already accordingly guided.

Whether this is spending time during the Lunar Cycles (Such as during the New Moon) to set intentions for your gifts and growth, along with other areas of your life, waking up every morning and setting intentions for your day, along with any other longer-term intentions you feel guided to set or ask for each morning, or otherwise periodically taking time to review or sit with what you'd like to ask for, and taking time to ask for it, please remember: *ask and you will receive*. If you would like to become a better channeler in the highest and best ways for you, *ask*. If you would like to become far more intuitive, *ask*. If you would like to live more intuitively, *ask*. If you are new to this, *try it*. If you are more seasoned, you already know what your process is, and know how to let it evolve if/as needed.

2. *Practice.*

You may laugh at the simplicity, however, practicing is a great way to get used to the state of being that you access when you channel. You can do this either through video, recording yourself channeling, using your intuition, such as through readings (tarot cards, etc.), or through any other means you feel called to use. You can also journal with some sort of consistency, daily, twice a week, etc. channelled messages for your highest good, about what's going on, about how life works, or anything else, really. The important thing is practicing, getting used to working with your gifts, and creating *easier access* to that which you already inherently are able to do, for your gifts will strengthen with intention, and through working with them further. If you are at a point where you are communicating with your guides, ask your guides how and when would be the best ways for you to practice, and don't be surprised if you begin being prompted to share your messages with the world. If there are messages you are meant to bring through for someone, The Universe, and your guides, will conspire to get that message through you and to that person, for the highest good.

Don't be surprised if the Universe presents you with opportunities to work with and expand your gifts for the highest good of others, either through bringing through messages for your friends, your family, (or even total strangers!), or otherwise by putting you in situations where using your gifts will be a boon to you, for if you are setting the intention, or putting it out there, that you would like to work with your gifts more, the Universe will conspire to put you in situations where you will be using them, and it won't let you fail either, for it knows just how to help you through these situations and won't put you through anything you're not ready to handle yet.

3. Meditate (Listen)

Setting aside time to connect, both with yourself, and with the higher realms, affords you a greater chance to listen to what your heart, your soul, your guides, and Source has to say. You do not have to follow traditional meditation practices, you do not have to find a waterfall to sit under, or a tall mountain to climb upon whereupon you meditate for 30 days straight. Whatever clears your mind, stills you, opens you up and provides you a chance to listen and receive information will suffice, even if it is just a bit of time alone by yourself. This is not to limit you, you do not necessarily need to be in a zen-like state to receive information, intuitively or channeled, from The Divine. However, what we are trying to convey is that a dedicated time to connect and listen, a ritual to signal commitment, however small, is a step that gives Source a greater opportunity to speak, and further signals your intention to your guides, to Source, to the Universe that which you are seeking. It is simply carving out time to receive, and affords further opportunity to talk to your guides, channel, and/or receive Divine information.

4. *Trust*

When you set an intention, when you are doing something you are meant to be doing, the Universe will very typically, if not always, show you some sort of confirmation or verification. Very frequently, when you channel something, The Universe will eventually verify this information you channelled. You can trust, especially as The Universe shows you, as The Universe, truly, is your teacher, that you will be shown at least some of the results of the work, and enough to build trust with The Universe and with your guides that the information they provide is accurate and correct, and that they will always channel through what is highest and best regarding the situation you are in, regarding who you are channelling for, and regarding the situation the recipient of the channelled messages you are channelling for. All contexts are considered. The Universe knows best. Your guides know, the angels know, and, of course, SOURCE knows. You can trust you will be shown the optimal ways for you, to channel, to utilize your gifts, and to work with the Universe.

Developing trust, with yourself, with your guides, and with The Universe at large, is a big step towards developing your gifts, as you will possibly find yourself in a situation where it is imperative to trust your guides, intuition, and channelling. Aside from that, there will be instances where you will be guided to speak up, to share what you know as a result of your intuitive and channelling capabilities, even if it is information that is different, or that many might not think it is possible to know, where you will know things you 'shouldn't' know, but that to you, will potentially be natural to know. Trusting your guides, and the process (and the Universe), will empower you to live life differently, more aligned, and to make some bold moves in the best directions for you. Your guides, and the Universe, will always pull through for you in the ways that are best for you. Your guides will know when to channel through you, and you may find yourself channelling, or at least relaying messages, for strangers or co-workers who have no idea that you are channelling. You may find yourself providing life changing advice, and, simply put, trusting the information you are receiving is a a big part of providing the impact that channelling and utilizing your gifts can bring to the table.

Furthermore, aside from trusting the information and your gifts and guides is trusting the process of your unfoldment and growth. You can trust that the Universe is guiding you along the best paths for you, and, moment by moment, it knows just where to lead you, just how your journey in utilizing your abilities can best unfold. Truly, you are guided through this process, and you have always been one with the Universe, have never been separate, and you have always been loved. Through all moments, The Universe has been there, and knows what you need, whether it be healing, grace, expansion, happiness, or anything else, in any endeavor. Please realize that all of life is underwritten and guided by the infinite intelligence of Source. Trusting Life itself, and your gifts, and the information you receive can lead to a bright and happier life, as you will know the answers that you need to know, you will receive what you need to receive, and you will realize you can trust everything, and in that trust, fear will diminish, and it will be easier to thrive.

Learning to trust the information you are receiving will also allow you to make leaps and bounds in living and leading your own life. You will have an easier time choosing for yourself what directions and endeavors you choose, and you will know (quite) a bit more about the people around you, what they need, who they really are, and what's really happening in the dynamics and situations around you. You will also be able to directly listen to what is occurring within you and your own heart, your *soul* as you go about your day and contemplate your life and potential directions for yourself. You will likely get direct answers to your inquiries in the first place, however, to explore around those answers will yield you even more accurate intuitive information that satisfies your need to ensure you're making the right choice for yourself.

You have never been alone. It may now be time to trust what your guides have to say, to trust what you are getting intuitively, to trust life as it unfolds, and to trust you, in whatever ways would be for your highest good.

5. *Persevere*

You can trust that your guides, angels, and Source, will open the pathways for you, will clear the road, so to speak, whenever you need it, and in what ways would be best. You do not have to fear. Life on Earth, while increasingly magical and synchronistic, can sometimes take perseverance in certain instances. You can trust there will be smooth sailing in many aspects, and that all things are taken care of, truly, and looked after. There are no accidents. At the same time, there are moments, circumstances, inner-work, or other scenarios that will entail perseverance and fortitude as you embark upon your journey. Things will be as things will be, however, if you wish to develop more fully, there may be instances where you will have to persevere and keep going. When things get tough, if they do, please persevere. Keep going. Keep practicing, even if it is more sporadic for a time, for there are things in life that can come up, and while your guides and angels will work with you, aid you, and hold space for you as much as they can, we still ask that you continue to show up, for yourself, for what you wish to develop, whether things unfold right away or take some sort of time and effort. The Message is, *keep going*. Things will open up for you. You are not alone as you embark upon this path. And don't forget to *ask for ease*.

6. *Believe*

Believe *you can do this*. You are Divine. Source is you and you are

Source. You are a beautiful light, and you are here to do great things. Please trust your magic. Trust what you get when you ask for your highest and best gifts, for you are inherently worthy of amazing things. Believe you are capable. Know you are, and trust the answers you get, trust the gifts you have. Trust your connection, and trust who you really *are*. You are a brilliant soul. You are here for a reason, and your gifts, and your intentions, can aid you in doing great things, for yourself and others, for the highest good, and in making an impact. The impact *you* are meant to have. Don't worry what others think, what they think you should be, for deep down, you can access and *know* who you are, and who you are *meant to be*. You are always you, and even if there comes a time where you must once again align with who you truly are, trust that you always can. You can always become who you were meant to be. It's never too late to be who you truly are.

You have all the support of the Divine, of the angels, of your guides, of all those who are with you for your highest good, and they couldn't be happier, prouder, of who you *really* are, and of *all the good* you have already done here, and *of all the great things* you *will do*, both for the planet, and for all. For each step you take, to align with who you really are, to *raise in vibration,* as they say, to ascend, to go further, to be more *you,* to shift and grow in the highest and best ways, also impacts the whole. As above, so below, as many say, as within, so without. To shift, expand, and evolve has an impact on all around you, on the planet, and on everyone. As you embark on this journey, as you *connect* more consciously, as you channel, as you talk to your guides, and learn to communicate with your guides, the angels, with Source, you bring forth more Divine energy, higher ways of being, higher levels of *consciousness* to the planet and those around you. Seeing as the Universe is infinite, there are no limits, and all is already accessible to you, and to all. As you step into all that is possible for you, you unveil possibilities to the all for their highest good, and allow for the infinite expansion of humanity and all there is to continue for the highest good. As you carry higher dimensional energies in your energy fields, you bring this higher way of being to all you encounter. As you expand, you open up doorways for others to expand, and as you become who you are meant to be, you have the impact you are meant to have on this planet automatically, just through being you.

7. *Know*

This may seem strange to you, that *know* is included in a list of practical methodology to expand your channelling. However, when you develop both your intuition and channelling, the ability to just <u>*know*</u> <u>*opens wide*</u>. You already have this ability, as all do. There are instances where you may find you simply have an instant *knowing,* like a flash of inspiration, or an action you take without thinking that turns out to be the 'right' one. When you *know* you simply know, like an intuitive flash, and as you get more comfortable with your gifts and knowing, you will find that this happens more frequently, and you can mix in your knowing with your channelling and intuitive capabilities to form a strong synergistic force of perceiving *well beyond* what many now think is possible. With all your gifts working in sync, you can truly become a force to be reckoned with. As you hone in your gifts, you allow for each gift to support the other, to help hone the other, and before you know it, you will find yourself developing and honing your amazing gifts in your own ways, in the ways that The Universe, and your guides, the angels, Source, and your intuition and *knowing* show you.

For again, we reiterate, there is a way that works best <u>*for you*</u>. It is your path, your choice, and it is up to you to walk it in the best ways for you, so to speak. The Universe knows what would be best for you, what series of events would help you, what practices, what ways to show up, what people, and what places, and, really, everything beyond that. Trusting in your path, and honing in on your *knowing,* and on your other gifts, truly, can be what brings you to the place *you* are meant to go to with all of this. *You know.*

This list is not extensive, but rather, a jumping off point, much like this book. It is up to you to walk your path, to heed your calling(s), and to *go* where it is you are meant to go, both in life and with your gifts. You are not alone as you heed these calls, as you embark upon any journey you go upon, for your guides are with you, the angels are with you, and yes, Source, The Universe, are always with you, for they are all. (Difficult to really be alone, we know.) So while we hope this list has been of service to you in the highest and best ways, and sparked ideas for you as you move forward, ultimately it is repeatedly showing up, setting those intentions, and moving forward that will bring you the results you inquire after. Trust it will show up. Take your inspiration, your motivation, and your *knowing* and move forward, even simply implementing one practice to move towards what you want. You are a powerful being, and you have the light with you, so call upon The Light, that is all and that you are, call upon your strength, and ask for the best outcomes, the best first steps, and trust the leap you take into an all new way of being on this Earth.

May your gifts expand in whatever ways would be highest and best for you, all for the highest good, should it be in the highest good. May you be blessed with the highest and best forward movement and practices for you regarding expanding your gifts, should it be in the highest good, that or better, all for the highest good. Amen. You are blessed.

Chapter 5

ENERGY

As we touched upon earlier, everything is energy, and as your ability to perceive things energetically opens wide, you open the door to combine your natural abilities to feel and read energies with your other gifts. With your intuitive capabilities, with your channelling capabilities, with your knowing, with your talking to your guides, and with your ability to perceive through the energies around you, you can further your awareness and abilities to an extraordinary degree. You are infinite and unlimited, and through all your senses, even if they go beyond what is spoken about in this book, and what is talked about in most spiritual and metaphysical areas of topic, you can truly hone in on who you are, and what you are truly capable of.

Seeing as Source is all, and everything is energy, it is possible to perceive beyond space and time quite easily, as energy operates beyond space and time. In fact, let's try something, as it is possible to step outside of time. We say 'let's try', because it is up to you and where you are at to feel it, the sensation of stepping out of time. How will we do this? We will do as we did earlier, and simply ask. Take a moment to sit quietly, and feel the space around you, feel the energies of how things are. Then, take a deep breath, maintaining that sense of awareness, and read the next sentence:

> *We ask that, should it be in the highest good, you, the reader, once you get to the last word of reading this sentence, are stepped outside of time in the highest and best ways for you, thank you.*

Take a moment to sit with that sensation, and know you can step yourself outside of time at any moment through intention... simply ask to be stepped outside of time, and there you will be.

We show you this simply to show you that, in a sense, *time doesn't exist.* It's all energetic, and you can *feel into,* energetically, something that happened 4 months ago, (or far longer) as well as future possibilities regarding choices you will make, or can make. You are beyond time. You are beyond space. You can *know.* You *do* know.

We point your awareness to energy, and quite soon, *energy work,* for through perceiving, feeling, in an energetic sense, you add another layer of awareness to your life and living, and to your work with your guides and channelling. Energy does not lie. When you feel the energy of a situation, you are feeling what is actually there. Add in intuition or any of your other similar gifts, and you can quite readily discern the truth of any choice or situation. Yes, you can create any energy you desire, you can be a pure conduit of pure energies from Source for the highest good, such as Reiki. Those who can sense things energetically are often drawn to crystals, energy tools, and other things that bring in good energies, or that allow them to experience more energetically beyond simply what many might call the mundane. (Though in truth, since Source is all, even the 'mundane' is quite extraordinary, is actually energetic, for all simply *is,* all is connected and energetic, and there is no true separation between the physical and the etheric. It is all one. Think layers.)

We spoke earlier in this book regarding energy, and how oftentimes when your guides speak to you you will perceive an energy of what is being communicated, as well as, potentially, the energy of your guides speaking through you, channelling through you. When you can perceive energy, both through feeling and *seeing,* you open up an entire world, that was always present, that allows you to go beyond where you were before, and have an entirely new level of impact for the highest good of yourself and those around you. For all your actions will then be guided by your energetic perceptions, and the actions you take, the intentions you set, will be energetic in nature, which will broaden the impact of the actions you take, of the words you speak, for you will be speaking to an inherent truth of what is there, and as you move energy with your thoughts, actions, and words, you will be able to set intentions that impact not just what you see right in front of you, but, in fact, the entire world, and Universe at large. For you are so much bigger than just a physical being on this planet, but are, in fact, infinite, with an ability to impact the entire planet with your intention.

So when you perceive energetically, and learn to work more consciously with the energies you are perceiving, and with energies channelled through you from the infinite, or brought forth directly from Source, through your intention, you are able to change and create regarding the fabric of reality itself. For you *are reality,* you are infinite, one with Source and all, and your intentions and ability to create and manifest in this world, and on this planet are *huge.* When you incorporate channelled guidance and intuition along with this ability to move energy, to channel energy, to do energy work, you become a *force of The Light* to be reckoned with. For what are spells and witchcraft but another way to move energy and/or create an outcome with intention? What are rituals but a focus for intention? You will find you are <u>so</u> *infinite* that the rituals are really just placeholders for you to *focus* your intentions, and the impact can be had and felt through pure intention alone, without the ritual, for *you are the magic, you are reality,* you are powerful. Ritual can serve other purposes, and, of course, there are multiple meanings for the word, but we speak here of rituals of intention and creation, and we tell you now, please continue to do what works *for you,* but know of the power regarding intention and energy *work.*

We speak of energy so much in this chapter because it can be of service in multiple ways. Perception of energy gives you an expanded awareness that you will always have as you open up to it further, for you are *all* energetically sensitive to some degree, and that degree can always expand as you awaken more to the truth of reality and what is around you and within you. Your awareness is so important as you progress, for it will tell you all it is that goes on both within and externally, and gives your guides more to speak to you about, and speak *through you* about when it comes to channelling and talking to your guides. It also allows you to become more familiar with the energetic signatures of your guides, of the angels, of Source, and how it *feels* when they speak to you, when they are around you, when they speak through you, for your perception and awareness will allow you to know who it is you are speaking to, who is speaking through you. You will know.

When all your senses combine, to work together, your intuition, your energy awareness and sensitivity, your channelling and your communication with your guides, you will become to a degree, very knowing, perhaps all knowing to a certain extent, for all of these things can expand the other, they all crossover with one another and combine to create a synergy of knowing that allows you to help others in the directions they go, in their healing, in any healing work you facilitate, and in developing their own awareness, in sharing any messages they need to hear in order to heal or transform in ways that would benefit all for the highest good. It will also help you in choosing your own direction, in setting your powerful intentions, in your own wellness, in whatever you need.

Another way to expand your wellness and other gifts is through energy work. Reiki has not only helped many to open up their energy sensitivity, but also unlocks and unblocks other aspects of one's energetic systems, gifts, intuition, channelling, and/or other capabilities, for it truly works only for the highest good and works on levels that not all modern medicine is intended to do, such as spiritually and energetically. Incorporating an energetic practice, whether it is Reiki, another modality, or simply a product of your intention, such as asking Source and/or the angels and/or your guides to energetically clean and clear your energy fields and do any energetic work that would be for your highest good, then sitting with the sensations of them doing that work for you, will expand your awareness, will aid you in balancing yourself in all facets of your life, and can further your understanding of intuition, of awareness, of energy and how it affects you and the world. Your ability to help yourself and others will expand, as the energy work, especially guided by Source and your guides, can potently impact all you encounter for the highest good. It can enhance your connection, strengthen your energetic systems and fields, and even allow you to become a cleaner channel, both of energy and of your guides when they channel through you. When you work with energy, you work with the core of what makes up your experience on Earth, and as such, it helps you to expand your impact, and empowers you to create change on an all new, higher level.

So we will provide for you now an energy work exercise that will allow you to expand your channelling, open you up further to your guides and angels, and allow you to experience your connection to the higher realms more concretely.

Please sit when you are ready, close your eyes, and connect with your breath, moving into a meditative state. Once you are there, envision, or, as we have spoken to, *ask,* for pure, loving, Source Light Energy to flow to you from Source, down to your crown chakra (located at the crown of your head), and let it flow down to your heart chakra at the center of your chest, and from there, let it flow out to the rest of your body for your highest good. Seeing as Source is infinitely intelligent, infinitely wise, it knows you, everything you've been through, where you are now in your life, where you are coming from, and it knows what you need most, and what would be most highly beneficial to you for your highest good, it knows just where this healing, loving Source Light Energy needs to go for you, and it will flow exactly where it needs to, working in just the right ways for you and your highest good, to aid you however would be best for you and for your highest, greatest good. Let the Light from Source expand, going wherever it needs to, flowing throughout your body, around you to your energy fields, and, from there, you can ask it, or envision it, flowing through-out your life and your living, to your relationships, doing whatever would be highest and best for you.

Source is unconditionally loving, it loves you and everyone, for it *is* all, you, and everyone, so it knows just what work would be most loving and best for all involved in any work you are doing. You can ask that all energy work you facilitate or do is only for the highest good, and trust that Source will only do the work that is pure and for the highest good of all, including you. When you are ready, or otherwise get the message that this exercise is complete, you may bring the session to a close however you feel so called, ground yourself (ask to be grounded), and sit with any experiences you had, jotting down any notes regarding messages or visuals you received while facilitating the energy work. Trust that the healing will continue for however long will be for the highest good, and you can further set the intention that the energy works for however long would be for the highest good, until any and all shifts and changes that would be for the highest good are completed.

Trust you are always connected to Source, directly, so this energy is *always* accessible to you. Furthermore, and similarly, seeing as Source is all, is the Source of all energy, you may ask for any other healing energy to flow from Source, through you and/or for you and/or your life with this exercise, including, but not limited to, Reiki, The Violet Flame, Angelic Light or any other energy you feel called or guided to ask for.

Running these healing, pure, high vibrational energies through your systems can further open you in the highest and best ways. It can and will boost your vibration, bring healing and clarity, clear up your systems in ways you may need, if you need that, or otherwise unlock gifts you may not have previously realized you had. You are always connected. You are one with Source and any and all energies and frequencies are, for the highest good, accessible to you from Source. For those more familiar with Reiki, or other modalities and forms of energy work, you do not need an attunement with these energies to work with them, you simply need only ask for them from Source, and they will be there. This is not to denigrate attunements, for they can be helpful, beneficial, and can be instrumental in large shifts for certain individuals, though they are not necessary to reach your full potential. They can be a boost, can make it easier to access certain frequencies and energies, such as Reiki, and they can elevate you and cause you to purge and clean house energetically all for the highest good, but you are not limited to needing an attunement, as helpful as they can be. Seeing as we have spoken of how these words in this book spark downloads, transmissions, and can facilitate happenings that are much like attunements to channelling for the highest good, we would say that if you feel so called to learn a modality such as Reiki or Valeyu-Mí, and find a teacher that resonates or that you feel guided to learn from, please do accept the attunements you are offered with those classes, should you be guided to do so. Please trust your intuition and your guidance systems. You are not limited, however, sometimes attunements and upgrades come to you and enter into your awareness and your life for a reason, and we would advise you to trust your intuition and guidance in accepting or going with these upgrades or attunements you are offered, such as through energy work classes.

Please trust your own intuition and guidance regarding energy and energy work, and move forward in whatever ways you feel called regarding this part of your journey and experience. You will develop your own understanding that works best for you as you progress and enhance your own abilities and awareness. Trust what you get and move forward, for so often energy work is guided intuitively, and when you work with Source, Reiki, or other infinitely intelligent energies that work for the highest good, such as Valeyu-Mí, these energies will only work for the highest good, which is a good starting point for working with energy.

Go forward knowing you have received whatever downloads and knowings, whatever transmissions, have been for your highest good on this topic as you read, and as those settle in, more realizations and deep knowings will spring forth for you. Thank you.

May you be blessed with the highest and best knowings of energy, energy work, higher dimensional being, and how best to incorporate energy work and energy awareness into your life, all for the highest good, should it be in your highest, greatest good, that or better. Thank you.

Chapter 6

KNOWING

Knowing is different than belief, as a belief can often be something handed you by another on a human level, while a *knowing* is inherent, is something you receive, is something instant and claircognizant, coming from a higher place, such as Source, The Infinite. We do not speak of a memorized fact, but rather, a knowing that comes to you or hits you instantly, whether it was something that others might think you 'should' know or not. What we mean is, if you are half-way across the world, then suddenly get hit with a feeling, or knowing, that something has happened for a relative or friend, perhaps you perceive their energies or the energies of an event that has transpired, or you simply *just know*, then find out later what you had known or felt had happened had indeed transpired, that is a moment of knowing, or the reception of knowing. Learning to trust your moments of *knowing*, such as through experience, like having the knowing hit, then later finding out you were incredibly on point, then recognizing that knowing hitting about other topics based on the similar feeling of those points of knowing *going* forward, is one way to develop your awareness and abilities of knowing and intuition as you evolve and progress with your abilities. We talk about knowing in this chapter for a way to enhance your communications with the Divine, your guides, Source, and the Universe at large is through your claircognizance and instantaneous knowings. It is another way for The Light to communicate with you.

An important point is that *you already know.* You are one with The Infinite, with Source, with all, and as such, the inherent knowing of *everything* is something you can access, as it is a part of you. Deep down, on *some level,* you *know*. Though, the *knowing* can be quite in your face, rather than something just deep down. You are infinite, Source is you and you are Source, and as such, the knowing is inherent, comes from a higher up place that is yet a part of you. You may at this time, have images or times in your life when you *just knew* show up for you, or pop into your awareness as you read. As you move forward, you may encounter a moment of knowing, then instantly get an image of this book, or of a memory of you reading this chapter. That could be one way your intuition tells you you just had a moment of knowing. As we spoke of earlier, learning to recognize when you are actively utilizing your gifts and abilities is one way to expand your working with them, for as you become more aware of when you simply just *know,* you will be able to trust and more often work with your inherent *knowing* and claircognizant abilities.

You are a beautiful soul, and with your gifts you have an ability to spread a lot of light through just knowing what to do, what to say, what's going on, and helping others to either access their own gifts, or get through a difficult (for them in that moment) situation when they need to hear words coming from a place of *knowing. When you channel, come from a place of knowing, work with intuition and other abilities, many people will sense that your wisdom is coming from a higher up place,* and as such your words can have *more* of an impact to those who sense that. For words spoken from a higher up place of truth can in fact, be felt energetically quite potently. We would like to, furthermore, speak to the energetic *downloads* and *transmissions* that come along with channelled messages, phrases, words, creations, works of art, symbols and languages, or anything else that is coming from a pure higher up place for the highest, greatest good of those who are receiving the message, or otherwise, coming into contact with the work, as well as the highest, greatest good of all. Being a conduit of Highest Light, The Divine, Source, and whatever else is of the highest light and for the highest good for you to be a conduit of can result in further healing, upgrading, relief, as well as many other beneficial outcomes for the highest good of you and those who you work with. Even those you pass by on the street benefit from your growth, elevation, and progress, for your energies, your progress, impacts the whole, and can be felt on an energetic level by *all* you encounter. Your inner work, your elevation, your highest and best evolution, all that you do and go through to go higher, to evolve in the best ways for you, all that The Universe provides for you to aid you in your spiritual development, can and does, in fact, impact far more than just the people you directly work with when it comes to utilizing your gifts and abilities. All around you, all you are connected to, benefit from your raise in vibration, your *elevation*. At the same time, you are also *all of it*. You have access to *everything*. You are *infinite,* you are *unlimited,* and can step into any space, any frequency, any dimensional energy or frequency that best suits a situation, so, in a sense, elevation is a term for refining the human aspect of your incarnation. You could say, you are already there.

Please trust your path, your direction, and the ways The Universe guides you to unfold and prosper in all areas of your life. You are divinely looked after and protected always, and you will see the results you are looking for if you keep going. You are infinite, and *all* is accessible to you if you ask, if you choose to step into that space of infinite knowing, of being the infinite you that you truly are. Please trust how things show up for you, how your *knowing* shows up for you, how *your gifts* show up and expand and evolve from here on out, for the infinite you, who you truly are, your highest self, knows *exactly* what is *best for you, and you are guided*. Learn your ways. Uncover your knowing more fully, and step into who you are *meant* to be, with the gifts and *abilities* you were created to have and use this lifetime for the highest good of all.

You are not alone, your guides are with you, *ready* to talk to you, expand your knowing, and aid you in evolving in the highest and best ways for you, both with your gifts and abilities yes, but also in whatever other ways would be best for you, even beyond the scope or range of what is discussed blatantly in this book, in these words, on these pages. You go so far *beyond* what many here have told you, and it is time for you to uncover the true you, who you truly are, *what* you are. With your knowing and awareness expanded, you can begin to see how far you truly go, how *beyond* you truly are. When you see the truth, when you know beyond any shadow of a doubt who you are, what you're here to do, you will then be able to live in full alignment with the highest, truest you. Of course, you can simply ask to do so and trust what follows, however, wouldn't the knowing of it also make it that much sweeter? Do both if you feel so called and/or guided. We wish you the highest and best blessings for your true knowing, for your expanded awareness of your knowing, and for being who and what you truly are, and being who you were born to be.

So step into your *knowing* in whatever timing and ways are best for you, and trust that The Universe and your guides will give you all you need in terms of experiences and confirmation to begin to open up to the full extent of your knowing and intuitive capabilities, in the timing and ways that are best for you, as well as any other spiritual and/or energetic gifts you choose to hone, or projects/endeavors you undergo.

May you, with ease and grace, be able to connect with your knowing in the highest and best ways, and live from a place of optimal knowing, whatever would work highest and best for you. That or better, thank you.

Chapter 7

TRUSTING

There will be times you are called to bring through information for others, especially at first, where you are *seemingly* going out on a limb, so to speak, where you will have to *trust* what you are guided to say and/or do. Such as, channelling about future events, or how things will unfold. It is important to establish a rapport with your guides, for while they are immediately all knowing and understanding of all that transpires, for you, it is important to develop trust with them, with Source, and with your intuitive and channelling capabilities, if you haven't done so already, for your sake. For trusting your intuition, which is always *right,* your guides and the information you are channelling for the highest good is important if you would like to truly make use of what you are bringing through, both for yourself and others. Once the Universe and your guides ease you into being more comfortable with trusting all that you receive, you will then be able to go on to do further extraordinary things, and make amazing choices based on trust and true faith that, otherwise, might have been more difficult to make.

Your intuition is a *tool*, a direct part of you, that you can work with to enhance both your own life, and the lives of others. Through this knowing, you truly can know everything going on around you, be *all-knowing,* in a sense. If you are newer on your journey, then you can trust you will get there in time, if you have not already uncovered these for yourself. The Universe will guide you through the steps you need to take to come into trust. You can trust life and the Universe will, one way or another, bring together the series of events, messages, people for you to help, people that will help you, etc. that will bring you into trust. *Especially if you ask.*

For The Light, Source, unconditionally loving, infinitely intelligent, infinitely wise, is all, is *in control.* It knows what's best for you, and especially if you ask for it, it will bring you, in the highest and best ways, all you need. This includes trust. Trusting your guides is a first step towards moving into spiritual independence, where, in a noisy internet culture, you will be able to cultivate your own sense of what's truly true for you. For when you learn to listen, receive your own information and downloads, upgrade and move forward on your own, in a genuinely connected, *knowing* way, you come into your own personal power regarding spirituality and knowing what's true. When you don't need someone else to tell you what to 'believe', you are able to uncover what's actually there, and you won't need to, necessarily, 'believe' when you can come into knowing and trust of The Universe and your guidance systems. For the Universe is constantly feeding you messages and information, both intuitively and through everything around you, for The Universe is you, is all that is around you, and, should you choose to pay attention, you too will notice how the Universe communicates to you all of the time. It is in learning to trust these signs, trust your intuition and how you read the energies around you, to trust both yourself, and all around you, that you become more capable of navigating all your surroundings with greater ease, grace, and peace. For in trust you find more peace, more love, less fighting, more surrender, for these things, this life, does not have to be difficult. You don't have to make things more difficult than they have to be, and, in fact, if you simply listen, you will come to trust all around you much more quickly, for The Universe is always speaking. Open your ears, open your eyes, and observe what is brought to your attention, observe what sticks out to you, what stays with you when you notice it, for what is a sign will be something you are meant to notice, something that sticks out to you. The Universe is always communicating. *Always.*

Learn to discern. In discernment, you will have greater ease in navigating that which presents itself to you in your awareness. There is so much more determining what shows up in your reality than what you see on the surface, so much *more* to reality itself than many speak of as of the time of writing of this chapter. Things do not work exactly in the ways, most likely, that you have been taught by others, however, it is possible to learn to discern what is not true, and what is. It is possible for you to see the truth. It is possible to come into deep understanding and trust of your guides, and the infinite, of Source, and of you. All of this, all of existence, is of the highest light and for the highest good. Even when people die, they go *home*. Seeing as time does not exist, space even, does not really exist, no one has truly left home, heaven, as some call it. For you are Source and Source is you, and you can not truly separate from that which is you, that which you are. So while the fears you may at times experience are from old genetic patterning, ancestral DNA and genetics, you do not need to come out of trust of The Universe, The Light, Source, for *all is looked after.* You are Light. Light is all. You can *trust.*

Be discerning and pay attention, however, when you consistently are provided accurate information from Source and your guides, (as information from your guides and/or from Source always is accurate), from the signs around you from The Universe, and are constantly shown the information you receive and provide to others from your channelling and guides is accurate, at that point it becomes pertinent to trust what you are getting, and to trust you really do have an amazing talent and gift that can help people. It doesn't matter what other information or agendas other people try to sell you compared to what The Universe tells and/or shows you, for The Universe is infinitely intelligent, knowing, and wise, thus, it knows better. Listen to your guides. Listen to what you're receiving, listen to The Universe at large. It knows best. Stay aware, keep discerning, stay on top of it, keep listening, yes, and at the same time, you have to trust. While some seek to control what's around them, they often do not stop to think that the atoms and molecules holding themselves together just so, the world staying in perfect orbital distance around the sun to maintain life, all these things that make life possible in the first place are out of their control, in a sense. The Universe is in control. Source is in control. Yes, you are powerful, more powerful than you think. Yes, you are amazing, infinite, unlimited, beautiful, and capable of amazing things, and it is important that you are incarnate and experiencing incarnation on Earth, and it is true you have a major impact by being there, being you, who you truly are, who you are meant to be. You are here for a reason. At the same time, you have to trust The Infinite Source of All, Life, in all its purity, in all its wonder, in all that it truly is, and trust the God-Given amazing abilities you have inherited this lifetime, that you get to experience having and utilizing hopefully for the highest good of all.

While you are infinitely powerful, you can trust the Universe has your back, in the best meaning of the phrase. It will not steer you awry, it will always come for you, bring you into balance when you need it, or bring you what you need, especially if you ask it to do so, or otherwise help you in the ways that you need. The Universe will never leave you hanging. To remain in communion with the Universe, to continuously trust and receive, listen to what it is telling you, you will learn so much more, on a deeper level, than you thought possible.

We remind you to look deeply when you look at what the Universe is saying. Look at the energy *underneath* things, beneath what is said by others, underneath the events and things around you. Can you see the *undercurrents?* Can you see what's *truly there, what is really being said?* Trust the answers you get, and if you need help understanding what is being spoken of here, please *ask for it.* See what you are shown, see what you get! You are intuitive, and in the right time, all these things spoken of in this book will be revealed to those of you who are ready to know what we are talking about here. Please trust that in the right time all of this will unfold for you in Divine Right Timing, for all is infinitely looked after by Source, which makes up all.

You are loved and necessary. Your timing in reading this book is Divine and perfect. Trust in the timing that The Universe has been working things out in for you, and in your life. The more you pay attention to timing, and looking at *why*, perchance, things you wanted sooner rather than later were delayed, or why things you weren't expecting came about so suddenly, and you will see that The Universe truly does know best for you and your life, and all the rest of the denizens of the Universe, and the planet and Universe itself. You are not separate from the all, you are one with all, so please trust us when we tell you, you are not forgotten, you are looked after, The Universe cares and you can trust even the small things are looked after in your life, down to the details of your shoe (and beyond).

Please let go of inhibition when it comes to trusting your intuition, for many of Earth's populace are still learning, still growing, still discovering what it truly is they are capable of as incarnate beings upon the planet you are living on. When you know, you know, so trusting what you are hearing, what you are seeing, what you are getting, even amongst those who don't **yet** see or hear quite to the level that you do is imperative to a more rapid growth and development. For as you trust, more opens up, like a solid foundation of trust and powerful channelling and intuitive capabilities ready to be built upon with further nuance in communication with your guides. Please trust that, should you ask it, and even if you don't, if it is truly meant to be, The Universe will bring you into trust, will conspire events to aid you in trusting for your highest good, with grace and ease, we request for you, for grace and ease will bring lightness to your heart and mind, a gentle expansion that is just right for you will make for a solid foundation which Spirit, The Light, Source, Your Guides, can build upon in a way that is just right for you and what you are meant to do here on this planet, why you were born here. Your soul knows, your guides know, The Light knows, Source knows, so please trust that if you haven't realized it yet, you certainly will in the years to come, for the unfoldment of life is uncanny in its ability to show you exactly what you need to see, to help you realize what you need to realize, etc. The Truth <u>always</u> comes to light.

We could go on, but time is drawing short as pertains to the scope and parameter of this chapter. Let's move on, shall we?

Many blessings of Trust for your highest good, in the highest and best ways, thank you! AMEN!

May you be blessed with optimal trust in the highest and best ways for you. Thank you Source, for bestowing the gift of trust to the reader in whatever ways would be highest and best for them, should it be in the highest good.

Chapter 8

DISCERNMENT

We request that you ask to effortlessly discern between messages from your guides, angels, and/or Source and your thoughts, telepathic messages you pick up on, and anything else. Ask for effortless discernment for your, and the, highest greatest good, then please trust what you intuitively pick up on when it comes to discernment for you, for it is your responsibility to discern. When you ask for ease, you will receive it, so we highly recommend asking for ease in any endeavor in your life, for greater ease with everything.

You do not need to fear any of what you encounter. You are Light, and only what belongs can come to you, especially if you set that boundary. Discerning is not about judging things around you, or becoming angry at what you see, when you see beneath the surfaces of what is presented to you by other people, by situations or groups. When you see the truth, you are able to see beyond what is presented and can see, feel, know, hear, and, heck, taste and smell the truth. At this point, the 'game' falls away and you can live life from a deeper level of understanding in what's going on. This is not to say your ego or other aspects of incarnate life will simply fall away over night as you embark on your journey, though perhaps for some of you major shifts will occur rapidly, but rather to tell you you will be able to more deeply discern what is happening around you. It is also important to practice discernment when it comes to your gifts and abilities and what you are picking up on. If you are newer it may take practice or The Universe bringing some lessons and events in alignment for you to fully come into your power and understanding around discerning what you are picking up on, but rest assured all will be made well, all will be made clear, especially if you ask. We do not say this to alarm you, but to tell you, if you are ever unsure ask your guides and the Universe to make it clear, and in the best timing for you, it certainly will be made clear what is, or was, going on at the time of your asking. Trust the feelings of the energies you get when you pick up on something intuitively, claircognizantly, or even when it comes to your channelled material and/or messages, for the energies don't lie, as we have said before. (And not just us.)

It is about looking beneath. Trusting what you're seeing. Not necessarily buying off hand what is spoken, but trusting what you feel and know in your heart to be true and light. Not everyone can see in the ways that you will be able to, so you have to trust where you are on your journey and trust what you get, what you receive. You are able to pick up on so much more than people in your life may readily tell you, accepting, of course, those who can channel for you or otherwise deliver a message from a higher level of consciousness and knowing. Even then, trust yourself. You are not alone in your ability to discern more accurately the truth of all that goes on, however, please utilize your own wisdom and discretion when it comes to any matter of importance, when it comes to any spiritual matter, or matter regarding your reality and the way you view the world. Be discerning regarding the input of the physical world around you, be it TV shows, people you talk to, or anything else, for that matter, though in truth so much of what you will choose as you connect with your spirit guides, Source, your heart and intuition, will be something you are guided to choose, something that draws you on a deeper level, and even if you choose something else, The Universe will speak to you through what you choose, one way or another. Since everything is Divinely Orchestrated, you never truly chose 'wrong', however, you can choose more in alignment with a higher path, the highest and best path for you. Your guides will aid you, your intuition will guide you, and everything will become easier as you flow with your guidance, so long as you are paying attention to what's in you, and what's going on around you.

You are not alone. Your guides will help you discern. The Universe will aid you in uncovering the highest and best truths for you, what truly *works* for you. Discerning is about paying attention, noticing what feels off, what feels on and correct, what is aligned and harmonized and what isn't quite there. You will know. You always know, and can connect with higher knowing to discern the truth of what someone says, of what you are reading, and of what is going on in the world. The more you pay attention, the easier it will be to discern. Active awareness breeds further discernment.

We remind you of the unfoldment of your journey, for if you are newer these things *will come* with time and some effort on your part, though please trust you are so guided and looked after as you undergo a spiritual development of any sort, and you may ask for further guidance, support, or anything else from The Divine at any point in your life. The refinement of your journey will allow for you to more clearly see from a purer place, less obscured by beliefs handed to you by others and coming more from a place of straight awareness, simple knowing. With this comes peace of mind, less struggle and fewer troubles in maintaining or fighting for a set of beliefs for any reason, not to say you will or won't have *any*, but simply to say you will be less inclined to buy a set belief from another, seeing as you can simply *know* things. Please trust the Journey, as The Universe is all, it knows what you are ready for, and what you are ready for next in your journey.

Speaking of The Universe, The Universe knows. If ever you have trouble discerning, ask the Universe to make it clear, and that clarity will show up one way or another. All is looked after. On a higher level, which you are a part of, all is well, all is as it should be. Trust the unfolding patterns, the new that is dawning on the planet, and know you will be looked after, your journey is known to the Universe, and you will not be overlooked. Discerning will become simpler once you have experience with picking out what feels true and aligned, vs. what feels fearful, ignorant, or regurgitated. You don't have to go along with popular sayings or beliefs when it comes to any sort of spiritual or religious culture, form of identity, or any other teacher or 'guru'. You can, in fact, go with what *you* are getting, with what works *best* for the true you. For you in your power will know what feels right, what feels aligned, and you will go with what feels best. You will follow your guidance in the best ways to a T, as the saying goes.

If at any point, for any reason, you look back, and realize you did not choose best, you did not go with what you had discerned or intuited, or did not go with your guidance, and your guidance was correct (as you will find through experience, it always is), you can simply take that as a lesson and gathered wisdom that you can take forward with you to aid you in choosing more in alignment next time you are faced with a choice between what you are intuiting, and something else. In this way, there's never a 'wrong' choice, simply a choice where you learn and take forward more wisdom for the future. This is not to say following your gut instinct, intuition, or messages from your guides would not have garnered you more wisdom, simply that at that moment in time, with where you were, you needed to make the choice that you did to learn what you needed to learn so that you could move forward in higher and better ways down the road. Your choices matter, but you can trust The Universe will bring you what is for you. You will move forward again from any circumstance. Trust. Make the best choices you can, ask the Universe for assistance, and trust that amends can be made from anything.

May you be blessed, in the highest and best ways, with accurate and optimal discernment, and the highest and best ways for you to discern. That or better, thank you.

Chapter 9

WALK YOUR PATH

There's a reason you are called to the things you are called to. You are meant to be you, the inherent gift and blessing that you are, with all the amazing ways that you work, with all the uniqueness and difference you bring by being who you truly are, by embodying your highest self, and harnessing all the amazing gifts and abilities you bring to the table to bring light to the world at large and those around you. You are a gift. You are meant to be you. You are meant to shine.

Even if there is some work to do, your calling beckons. Who you are is *amazing,* and we do not mean who you *think* you are, but rather, who and what you *truly are.* You are light, you are brilliant, and it is up to you, to open yourself to *truly discern* from a higher place the truth. We are not saying, necessarily, to go with what you think, but rather, what you *get,* what you *know* from a pure, higher place, if not the highest place, for you are already *all of it,* a powerful creator and manifester, one with Source, one with all, and it is up to you to *awaken,* realize it, own it, and move forward in your integrity, with your *true knowing and inner/higher wisdom.* Your thoughts can be divinely guided, can be telepathic in nature, can be important and leading you somewhere, so trust what you see and what you are getting, however, be mindful and aware, pay attention, and The Universe and your guides will take care of showing you the truth. We urge you to realize you are already aware, you already know when what you say isn't in alignment with truth, and when it is, for you are already far more aware than many on this planet have taught you to realize. However, you can now unveil the truth, uncover your knowing, and **know better.**

Your path is unique to you, so heed the calling of your own true path, heed the knowing that is within you, heed your highest guidance and wisdom. Others may try to sell you their agenda, their path, their ways which may or may not work well for you on your journey, but in truth, you are directly connected to Source and infinite knowing and highest wisdom, and highest light, you are Divinely guided, especially if you choose it, and you already have what you need within you. Why then seek guidance from a 'guru' who may or may not be coming from highest wisdom, who may or may not want you to shine brightly on your own without them? Why not instead seek the council of the infinite highest wisdom that is everything and knows everything and the how's and why's of how everything operates, that is you, and which you have direct access to? There will be those in their integrity, acting as conduits of the highest light for the highest good who will readily aid you, befriend you, help you to be the bright shiny you you truly are. There will be those who will aid you on your path to self-discovery and healing. You will have friends, you will not be alone in this lifetime should you choose it. Tap into your guidance and *discern* with ease the difference between the two as you travel along your experience here, experiencing all you are meant to. You will know. You always have the ability to do so, to know *everything*. So please trust what you are getting.

We tell you all of this so that you are aware that you must stand in your truths, in your power, walking your path, your calling, unafraid, trusting, and in tune with highest wisdom, with pure awareness and consciousness, with Source, knowing and fully aware of what is occurring to the best of your abilities, and you *can do that*. Maintain awareness. With your awareness you can discern what occurs around you and within you. You will never truly be left alone in the dark, for you will be able to discern your way back to the light at a moments notice, and with the right people around you, it becomes ever easier to be yourself, supported, with ease and grace around you and in your life.

As you walk your true calling, as the true you, who and what you truly are meant to be on this planet, you call to you all that is meant for you. The right people, the right experiences, all you need, all that is meant to be experienced by you. You are supported, you are here for a reason, you are blessed, and you will be abundant as you step into your role of who you truly are, who you are meant to be, doing what you are called and meant to do. It will come naturally as you evolve, as you become accustomed to doing and being in the ways the true you is meant to, is called to, at a soul level. You will feel it within your heart and soul, the very core of your being, from a higher place, and within you. You will know. Please trust that all the support you need to walk your true soul calling, to live and experience life as the true you, is readily at hand. All you need do is *ask*. You are meant to do great things, and you alone know the true depth of that saying as you read those words, you will feel and be drawn to what those great things are, each of you who read this individually. For these channelled messages have done more than provide words on pages for you, whether printed on paper or displayed on a screen, they have in fact, provided energetic transmissions that have worked for the highest greatest good, individually, for each of you who have read these pages, whether four words, ten paragraphs, or every last inch of each page. You have received what you have needed to receive, to open you in the highest and best ways, only for the highest good, to your guides, angels, and to Source, to your channelling and intuitive capabilities, and to any other gifts and/or aspects of you that would be in your, and the, highest greatest good to be unveiled and further accessed by you. You are amazing. Please *know* it.

As you walk your *true path,* you manifest all you need. Things fall into place quite easily, however, you do not need to take our word for it, especially as you hear from your own guides or higher self, you will receive the messages and truth of your situations, of you heeding your call, your unique call which is for you. You are here for a reason. Trust what you get please.

So please be *you,* who and what you *truly are,* and receive now all the downloads, boosts, upgrades, that would be for your highest good at this time to do so, should it be in your highest good. Simply ask Source to bring these things to you, right now, for Source is infinite, and you are infinite, and you can receive any upgrade, attunement, any download that would be for your highest good at any point in time, for all is available from Source, the Source of all, including all energies. Simply asking opens the door. You are you for a reason. You are here for a reason. Trust what you get when you ask, and trust who you become as you move forward intentionally, consciously, aware, expanding, evolving, and growing into who you are called to become. Through asking, awareness, and action, following your guidance, you can do anything you set out to achieve, and/or are guided to go for. Life has many gifts to offer you, especially as you step into all that you are meant to be, and do what you are called to do. You already know. Please trust.

We want you to own who you are, to trust in your guides, intuition, and guidance, for being who you are, and trusting in your true guidance systems will lead you optimally on your optimal path, through optimal life experiences for you, and what's more, you will *understand* from a higher level, you won't be torn up by certain experiences, or as afraid, if at all, by world events, by what is occurring around you, for you will *know.* You will know who you are, what you are doing, and why, at least to a degree that will bring you *enough* confidence to stand tall in truth, and in what feels optimal and correct, in what you are getting. And, if you are reading this, *you are so special and amazing.* You wouldn't be reading this if you didn't feel called to something higher, if you didn't have an innate gift and knowing to access and take you higher. We are pouring so much love into your existence now, as you read, as you realize, whether slowly or quickly, who you are, why you came here, and what you're all about. That *download* is inherent in these words, all for your highest good, so as the days, weeks, and months ahead come, watch out for any realizations, knowings, or messages, whether from your guides, in your thoughts, or in The Universe around you (and it will all be tied together for you at some point soon after all the messages) about who you are, about what you're about, and pay attention to how you *feel* about certain people, places, or things, for what is significant will stand out to you in some way, shape, or form, and once you have fuller access to your guidance, which you may already have, you will be able to verify this quite readily, and move forward like never before with accurate information. Please trust. Trust *you*. *You already have all you need*. The Universe will take care of the rest.

As you go forward, as you meet more people, have your impact, realize your own true value and worth, you will begin to open to new truths, new paradigms, higher ways of being, higher vibrations, and you will be *guided* and *looked after* through it all. Furthermore, you will shed all that isn't you, all that does not belong, from you, your perspectives, and from any beliefs that you were handed as a child, and become more highest aligned. For as you walk your path, the truth is unveiled, the old falls away, and what's left is you. You are all. You are infinite. That does not mean there are not ancient human patternings to unravel, which are healing at a rapid rate anyways, but rather that you get to experience this awakening, this unfolding, this existence and experience on Earth, and you get to come from a higher perspective while doing so. You are Divine. You are incarnate. So who, truly, are you meant to be as an incarnate being on this planet? Who, truly, are you? Let the Universe show you, for it will if you ask, if it hasn't already.

Should it be in your highest good, may you walk the highest and best path for you to walk, you being you, the authentic you, who and what you truly be, easily and with grace, love, and joy. May peace flow to you along your path at all times for which it would be in the highest, greatest good. You are infinitely blessed, and your path is an important one. We are sending you blessings to aid you in getting fully on your path, and walking it in the highest and best ways, in all ways that you can. You are fully supported in your life's journey, mission(s), and optimal, highest and best path. Thank you Source for showing the reader and blessing them with their optimal path in the highest and best ways. That or better.

Outro

THANK YOU

Thank you. We hope these messages and transmissions have found you well, or will help you to find yourself well in due time. May your guidance grow and expand brilliantly in leaps and bounds, in the highest and best ways. May your gifts and abilities evolve amazingly in the highest and best ways. May all the highest and best blessings for you be bestowed upon you now, from Source, for your highest, greatest good, in whatever ways would be for your highest greatest good at this now moment as you read this, or as this book exists in your proximity, that or better. May you expand in whatever ways would be *best* for you, and move forward in whatever directions would be highest and best for you, in the highest and best ways, should it be in your highest good. You are a blessing. You are a gift. Please know that now. Know you are not limited. Receive now the transmission in this outro, to aid you in the highest and best ways regarding what you received from this book, in finalizing anything which would be for the highest good to be finalized, or otherwise, in moving forward from here in the highest and best ways for you to do so. This is never limiting you, but is, rather, providing you the highest and best energetic send off as you progress onward. Of course, you may reread these pages for any more downloads or information that you are called to come back for, for Source, The Universe, will always provide to you what you need in the moment, what would be highest and best, that or better, as you read this channelled material. Even having this book near you, you can receive what would be highest and best for you to receive from it, for the the energies, and transmissions, can occur simply upon your request, or by having the book around you, in a space that you occupy. This makes this more than just a book, but an energy tool as well. This is all only for the highest good, in the highest and best ways.

May the highest and best find you, and may this book be of the highest and best service to those it encounters, for their highest, greatest good, and *the* highest greatest good.

We wish you highest love, peace, prosperity, and abundance in the highest and best ways for you, and all the highest and best connection and guidance for you. We wish you well in your journey onwards, with all the highest and best possible for you. Thank you.

Thank you for existing.

Thank you for being here.

Thank you for being *you*.

You are blessed. You are supported in the ways that are highest and best and for your highest good. You are loved endlessly and eternally. Go forward in the highest and best ways.

With the highest love,

Brandon and Xorbítal

Further Information

THE SYMBOL ON THE COVER

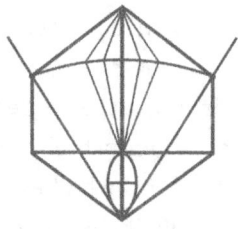

If you were wondering 'what the deal is' with the symbol on the cover, do we have some news for you! Brandon has been channelling through symbols for a language/healing modality currently named Valeyu-Mí. The symbol on the cover, the name for which is Vustá, means "Channel Prep", which is to say, encountering that symbol, should it be in the highest good, activates its energies for you, or whoever encounters it, and prepares them to channel in the highest and best ways for them. It opens the recipient up to channel, and prepares them, moves any energies that need to be moved, or, otherwise, works in the highest and best ways to allow them to channel in the highest and best ways for them. You could think of it as an upgrade, a boost, or a tool to utilize if you are preparing for a channelling event or session, should it be needed. The effects are only for the highest good, and work for the highest good in each situation and and regarding each being respectively, as the modality is infinitely intelligent and wise, and the energies come from Source, the energies will work or activate in the best ways for them to do so in each instance, moment to moment, however would be best and for the highest good.

This provides, in a sense, a double whammy, as those who read the book receive not only Vustá's effects and energies, but the transmissions and downloads from Source that are found with the channeled material and the book itself. If you bring in the additional channelled intentions, and blessings that can be found at the end of each chapter, you encounter a synergistic approach, along with the information found within this book, to truly give the reader or being encountering this book a boost, upgrade, activation, or whatever else they may need that would be for the, and their, highest good. Perhaps the word, 'overkill' will come to mind for some, however, we truly wanted to ensure this book would make an impact for the highest good of those who encountered it, read it, or were, otherwise, seeking to move further along in the highest and best directions for them in their spiritual and life paths. In truth, this is more than just a book. It's an energy tool as well, and it works only in the highest and best ways, for the highest good, including yours, should it be in the highest good. So thank you for trusting your guides and guidance regarding reading this book.

Additional Symbols

The 'X' with 4 lines around it and a halo found at the start of each chapter is a symbol for Xorbítal that showed up for Brandon as he was chanelling Valeyu-Mí symbols one day.

The symbol at the start of the next few sections is Valeyu, one of the Valeyu-Mí symbols.

Further Offerings

SESSIONS, LESSONS, READINGS

If you feel so called, you can find more information regarding Valeyu-Mí at Valeyu.com.

You may also reach out to Brandon regarding readings, channelling sessions, and energy work sessions through brandonhbloom.com.

Blessings

A Parting Gift

May you be blessed in the highest and best ways for you to be blessed. May the highest and best love, grace, peace, ease, abundance, and prosperity and highest connection occur for you, in the highest and best ways for you, should it be in your highest good, that or better. May you be blessed with all you need, and better. May you know who and what you truly are, and experience the joy of being who and what you truly are. May you see the blessing that you are, understand the gift that you are. May you experience what brings you true joy in this lifetime, what fills you up in the highest and best ways, what you are passionate about and what it is you are truly meant to be and do. May you find clarity and ease wherever and whenever you need it, and may your gifts and blessings unfold bountifully and beautifully for you as you move forward, this moment onwards, that or better. May you find confidence with your gifts and abilities in the right timing for you as you move foward on your journey/in your experience. May what is best for you always find you with grace and ease. You are infinitely blessed in the highest and best ways, should it be in the highest good. All is Divinely timed.

All is Divinely blessed and looked after, as are you. You are infinite.

Should it be in your highest good, go forward in the highest and best ways for you to do so, with grace and ease, free, confident, potent, powerful, and Divinely Guided in the highest and best ways.

That or better, all for the highest good.

Amen.

Xorbítal

Acknowledgements

(From Brandon)

A huge thank you and great love to all my guides, Xorbítal, the angels, archangels, Source, and those of the highest light and here for the highest good who guided me through the process of putting this book together, and an immense amount of gratitude and thanks for all of the other guidance you have provided.
Thank you. Thank you. Thank you.

A gigantic thank you to all who have helped me throughout my experience here on Earth this lifetime. Friends, family, teachers, mentors, and The Universe at large. It may all be The Universe, however, there is so much to be grateful for regarding all that occurred for this book to be here in your hands right now. Thank you to all that occurred throughout all of existence for this book to come into existence in the way that it is, right now. Thank you.

A big thank you to the trees who lived their lives, who's material are now a part of the pages of the print versions of this book. Thank you for all you have contributed to this world, through your energies, through your existence, and through your ancient wisdom.

Thank you to all the people and work that allows for this book to be out in the world!

Thank you for the world and Universe in the first place!

Thank you for existence.

And thank you, dear reader, I hope you get the best for you regarding this book.

About the Author

Brandon H. Bloom

Brandon is a channeller, energy worker, and intuitive with a huge passion for aiding people in the highest and best ways he is guided to. Having discovered a knack and love for energy work, channelling, crystals, and speaking and working with angels and spirit guides in 2017, he has since been certified as a Reiki Master/Teacher, founded a modality he received, Valeyu-Mí, for which he is currently teaching classes, and has helped numerous people through his classes, intuition, channelling, guided meditations, and energywork sessions. For more about Brandon and his work, please visit BrandonHBloom.com

www.ingramcontent.com/pod-product-compliance
Lightning Source LLC
Chambersburg PA
CBHW071026080526
44587CB00015B/2523

* 9 781735 586694 *